Laughter Lines

Life from the Tail End

Take a life with a small dog in tow, add a dash of red hair dye, a selection of crumbling biscuits and a passion for recitable verse... The result is a recipe for laughter. Sue Vincent shares her world in verse.

Laughter Lines

Life from the Tail End

Sue Vincent

Blame Diana...

Contents

From the small dog

(With apologies to Lewis Carroll)

"The time has come," the doglet said,
"to talk of many things;
Of tennis balls and squeaky ducks,
and sneaky bees with stings;
of why the sparrows fly so fast
and if that cat has wings."
"Just wait a bit," the writer said,
"I'm busy with these things."

"But writer," said the small dog then,
"The sun will shortly set,
the pheasants will be playing out,
and rabbits too, I bet.
I really should be practicing,
I haven't caught one yet."
"Hmm. Never mind, it's raining
and you don't like getting wet."

"Ok then," sighed the little dog,
"We could consider, please,
the therapeutic benefits
of sharing Cheddar cheese.
Or why that spider's sitting there.
Or why do you have knees..."
"You scratch a lot," the writer said,
"You sure it isn't fleas?"

The clouds were turning dusky pink,
Upon the fading blue.
The writer sighed, put down the pen
another task was through.
"Come on, small dog, go get the leash,
your walk is overdue."
The small dog answered sheepishly,
"Tough luck, I ate your shoe."

Ode to a Dead Office Chair

My dignity is damaged
Since the wheel fell off the chair
And sent me spinning backwards
With both feet up in the air.

There was that awful moment
When I knew I couldn't stop
And wondered on which bit of me
The chair ...and me... would drop.

I don't do acrobatics
...Voluntarily... these days
The passing years and dodgy joints
Have made me mend my ways.

The wrist took most of the assault,
The hip most of the rest,
The dodgy spine did none too well...
The chair had come off best.

I lay there winded, wondering
If I should dare to move
And if I did I wondered
Just how painful it might prove.

The small dog had a panic
And ran over in alarm
To check to see I was okay
Or if I'd come to harm.

She didn't know quite what to do,
But, glad I wasn't dead,
She licked my face and just sat down

To guard the corpse instead.

The corpse looked at the ceiling
Feeling rather wan and faint...
Deciding it could do with
Yet another coat of paint.

My dignity is bruised today...
My posture's not terrific.
Let's say I need a cushion...
And let's *not* be more specific...

So signing off with poetry...
A ditty, not an ode...
I plan to spend the afternoon
In horizontal mode.

Adventure

The fence has blown down with the wind and the rain
And with a small dog that's disaster,
A cat lives next door
And between them, it's war,
As we wait to see who can run faster.

The cat likes to sit on the roof of the shed
While the dog views this as an intrusion,
It's all fur and teeth
As the dog growls beneath
And the birds flutter round in confusion.

Now it's all very well when there's distance between
And the pair, by a fence separated,
But take it away
And there's hell to pay
As the cease-fire zone is negated.

I blocked up the hole in the fence best I could
But the small dog can wriggle right through it;
And chases the cat
At the drop of a hat
And if caught, I've a feeling she'd chew it.

So I shored it all up so the hole's out of sight
And I left the cat nowhere to hide,
But the wind howled all night
And though bolted up tight
The ruddy gate blew open wide.

'Course, I didn't notice the insecure gate
That stood open just as the wind blew it;

So I opened the door
And I thought nothing more...
While she spotted the gate and ran through it.

'She's quiet', I thought, 'playing out all alone,
I'll go out and perhaps have a look...'
And then came the fright...
Not a small dog in sight,
But I see the escape route she took.

I dive back in the house, grab the leash and the ball
And I wonder just how far she'll run,
And if she meets the cat...
No don't think about *that*...
Gawd, I hope that she's safe, having fun...

You worry so much when they're out of your care
And I'm kicking myself for my fault
But as I step outside
She is there, grinning wide,
As she skids to a jubilant halt.

Her smile says it all; you can tell she had fun...
She is bouncing with glee, I'm a wreck!
She wanders back in
Wagging tail, impish grin
To collapse in a heap on the deck.

An hour or two later she scratches the door
She's recovered but in for a shock,
'Cause she heads for the gate
But alas, it's too late,
I've installed her a nice shiny lock.

'The moral?' you're wondering, 'Isn't there one?'
Says the dog, 'Yes, a simple one too.

Take the moment at hand,
Live it full, and unplanned,
Lest the padlock be fastened for *you*.'

A Dog's Dinner

We had porridge for dinner, the small dog and I,
She likes it with cream on, I wouldn't know why...
She'd already eaten, but doing her duty,
Protecting my waistline and small claim to beauty,
She thought she'd be helpful and have second helpings
Distracting me nicely with wagging and yelpings,
And soon as my back was turned dinner was eaten,
I'm fast, but a hungry small dog can't be beaten.
She polished her own off and while I did dishes
It seems that a fairy came, giving her wishes
I *had* left my dinner in reach, it is true,
(An obvious failing, between me and you)
The ham disappeared without leaving a trace
Except for the grin upon one small dog's face
And so we had porridge, the doglet and I,
I can't say I fancied it, heaven knows why,
And then when I left it, you wouldn't believe it,
The small dog sneaked up and decided to thieve it.
It's my own fault, I know, a fact I can't ignore,
While *she's* fast asleep, all curled up on the floor.

Done

I've finally decided
I am glad I am so short,
The floor today seems way too far...
I really think it ought
To realign its distant stance
and do its best to meet me
About halfway twixt here and there's
the best place it could greet me.

I've done my back again, you see,
and have to blame the cat,
The ginger one next door
has provocation right off pat...
And hissing at the small dog
as we exited was bound
To set the small dog chasing,
as she ran the thing to ground.

All very well and natural,
for cat and dog to play...
For nature has designed
their animosity this way.
But I was holding grimly
to the small dog's lengthy lead
When she set off at speed
without the slightest bit of heed.

She hasn't got a clue, of course,
about inherent risks
And doesn't realise
she's playing Frisbee with my discs,
I dangled as she raced along...

from the 'controlling end'?
And so today I'm stuck with bits
that now refuse to bend.

I went to work this morning,
groaning all the ruddy way
To find we have appointments
in the town later today.
So I'll be lugging wheelchairs
when I feel I should be in one,
And wishing someone would invent
a really lightweight tin one.

The dog, of course, can't understand
why she's not had her run.
She really wants to go and chase
some more stuff in the sun.
The day is warm and casting
golden shadows on the wall...
But me, I want a nice hot bath,
and not to move at all.

It was all going so well too...

A lovely day had come and gone
As good as you could get;
I woke to silent darkness,
But I wasn't moving yet!
I'd wait till the alarm went off
And get a duvet fix,
I didn't want to start the day
Till after half past six.

The world was frozen, stark and clear
All inky black and white;
It could be worse, the forecasters
Had warned of snow last night.
The small dog chased her steaming breath
Beneath the frosty trees,
I huddled in the icy wind
That whistled round my knees.

Back home the heating had gone off
Without the least excuse,
The dog decided she'd be sick...
It might have been a ruse;
She doesn't like the back door shut
Needs access hail or shine,
And throwing up would put the door
In her control, not mine.

She's sitting on the doorstep
With her head outside the door.
The days unfold, you never know
What Fate may have in store.
Quite soon I find the sofa

Has become a small-dog den,
She looks at me pathetically...
And then throws up again.

I freeze and think of vet bills
'Cause I have to get her well;
She probably needs cuddles,
So I figure what the hell,
We'll have a lazy afternoon
And just curl up together,
There's nothing wrong with small dog hugs
In warm or winter weather.

I freeze at the computer screen
And launch on the attack,
The keyboard rattles busily...
Until it freezes back.
Eight hundred words have disappeared...
There is no saving grace
When 'safe mode' wipes the files
And they are gone without a trace.

But... time for work. I scrape the car;
The frost is cold and thick,
My fingers turn to indigo
Although I'm scraping quick.
A good five miles of empty road
Lies silently ahead...
And two miles in my little car
Gives up and goes for dead.

The power's gone, she's all puffed out,
And just won't move at all.
I plead and coax... reluctantly
She manages a crawl.
My son is waiting patiently

For breakfast to arrive;
The little car takes one last heave,
Collapsing on his drive.

She'll have to stay there now, of course,
The garages are shut,
And any travelling will be
By taxi or on foot...
And every taxi into work
Takes half my daily rate.
A duff PC, a poorly dog,
A dead car... f***ing great!

'These things are sent to try us'
So the ancient sayings tell,
Though given half a chance I would
Consign 'these things' to Hell.
But as I can't, I'll simply shrug
And raise a festive glass;
I'll cock a snook at destiny
And say, *'This too shall pass.'*

The Canine Diet

Its cream cheese and crackers for me and the dog,
While I'm more the epicure... she's just a hog...
I nibble quite delicately, don't you know,
She swallows the ruddy things all in one go.
While I take my time with the texture and flavour,
Enjoying the moment as something to savour,
She's sitting there watching as if it's a crime
That I am not sharing enough of the time.
She knows very well that although she's had dinner
Those puppy-dog eyes mean she's onto a winner...
If I don't give in to the piteous whine
She stares with a look that says plainly, 'It's mine.'
She's partial to emmenthal, cheddar and brie...
(and anything else on my plate she can see!)
It's all very well but my diet is meagre
And gets even less with a canine so eager
To filch every possible crumb from my plate....
Pretending somehow that its weeks' since she ate.
It's serious stuff this, 'cause I'm getting thinner
Not only because she is sharing my dinner,
Expending more calories than I am eating
(Though that might improve now the guy fixed the heating)
Does she share her dinner with me? Not at all...
Just laughs and insistently fetches the ball.
Perhaps I should patent this new canine diet
Instead of just sitting here keeping it quiet
'Cause in our society few things seem bigger
Than getting a handle on keeping your figure.
And people spend thousands on image and taste...
When it's simple... a small dog is good for your waist.

A Summer Night

The dog is laying at the door
I can't blame her at all...
It's hot tonight and thunder flies
Are covering the wall.
She's wearing fur, I can't complain
I'm robed in flimsy stuff
This little scrap of cotton robe
Is still more than enough.
She hasn't been too well today
And had a poorly tummy...
She snuggled up despite the heat
And seemed to want her mummy..
Myself, I think it's just a ploy,
Despite insistent licking...
And all the noxious gas attacks...
She's only after chicken.
I fed her chicken for her tea
And gave her ice cream too..
So suddenly she's full of beans
And bouncing round anew...
I really am a sucker
For this sneaky little pup,
She knows I'll go that extra mile
If I think something's up.
With big brown eyes she winds me
Round her paws with utter ease...
If all else fails she grins at me
As if to say. 'Aw,please..."
I just give up, she always wins
With such a loving glance.
This whirly girl can melt my heart
I never stand a chance!

Gardening

I've been in the garden the whole afternoon
And most of the evening too,
It's taken advantage while I convalesce
And could probably feed a small zoo.

Don't think I'm complaining, I'm loving the green
But I wouldn't mind seeing the flowers,
It doesn't take long for the weeds to invade
And I fought with the bindweed for hours!

I'd started, of course, with the overgrown lawn
And launched my attack with the mower,
It was wet, so I can't say I've done a good job
But at least the damned stuff's rather lower.

I'm only halfway through the job as it stands,
But it is one that is giving me pleasure.
The first summer flowers are starting to bloom
So you could say I found buried treasure.

The small dog, of course, chose to help me to dig,
In a place I did not want a hole,
If she gives up her role as a small blogging dog,
She could make a new life as a mole.

I gathered the toys she had left in the rain
And took then inside to the washer,
But if I find any more half eaten plants
I shall sit on the small dog and squash her!

Red for Danger

A bit disappointing I said to the glass,
It's not really orange, it almost has class...
It's still bright and vivid, I have to concede,
But a rather more virulent shade's what I need.

You've guessed it, I've been at the bottle again,
No, not 'mother's ruin', just dyeing the mane...
The dog thinks it's funny and raises her brow
You can tell that she's wondering what I'm at now!

My usual colour was not on the shelf
Let's go for adventure, I thought to myself
Selecting a box that looked several shades lighter,
In hopes of a beacon to make the day brighter.

A date with the scissors was next in the diary,
I'm growing the stuff and it looked a bit wiry,
So dig out the meat shears and hack away quickly
(A sight to leave any *coiffeur* feeling sickly).

It could be much worse, for it doesn't look bad...
(Well... better at least than a scouring pad).
You can cover up much when your hair is so curly
And even a massacred mop can look girlie.

I didn't want smooth hair, or ringlets or dreadlocks,
Just something that's easy to do with my red locks,
You could call it wild but that sounds a bit dressy,
It's probably fairer to just call it messy.

I might call it 'windswept', 'cause that's a bit nearer,
"You cut it yourself, dear?"... it couldn't be clearer,

Though auto-coiffure may appear a bit scary,
Hairdressing is by definition quite hairy.

So pass me the scissors and don't be alarmed,
Even though you may panic to see me thus armed
But hell, I don't care... you can just call it bed-head...
And take my advice... never mess with a red-head.

So which way is up?
Do the stars swim overhead
Or are we swimmers?

Saturday morning blues...

My son said, 'Happy accident?'
While looking all askance,
As sunlight streamed upon
The object of his startled glance

The supermarket shoppers
Milling through the crowded hall,
Had also lifted eyebrows
At the bobbing fireball.

I'd wanted something coppery
With sunny summer hues,
But there were just too many packs
I couldn't really choose.

I hummed and ha'ed and dithered
Till I had a choice of two,
But wasn't really in the mood
And just thought 'This will do."

Now something like a lion's mane,
In such a vivid red,
Defies control and radiates
In flames around my head.

The moral of this story, girls,
Is one both deep and true...
Never purchase hair dye
When you feel a little blue.

For a Bacon Sandwich

I'm just a tad bored with my diet,
There's nowt wrong with yoghurt *per se*
And I know that it's good for my innards,
But you don't want it three times a day.

The antibiotics are awful,
Make me ravenous morning till night,
I'm fair pittled off
With no vittles to scoff
And I'd kill to have something to bite.

I dream of a nice bacon sarnie,
On thick buttered bread, golden brown,
A crispy fried egg nestled in there,
And bright yellow yolk dripping down.

Just a couple of nicely cooked rashers
As ambition, it isn't that big...
It's taking the biscuit,
I daren't even risk it,
Yet look like I ate the whole pig.

A nice bit of rump steak would do it,
With cognac and mushrooms and cream,
And a small glass of Burgundy with it?
Ah well, lass, at least you can dream...

It is all bland and boring at present
As I wait for the duff bits to heal
And look forward with glee
To the day I am free
To indulge in a heavenly meal.

Rewriting the wrinkles

Oh give me a life on the open road!
With my dog and a caravan..
Just my books, paint and turps and a canvas..
And skin with a leathery tan.

Oh find me a place on a mountain!
Where the clouds can come down to play,
And the cold stream can ripple with laughter,
And no-one to find me all day.

Oh give me a hole in a hillside!
A warm, womb-like, bat ridden cave,
And skyclad I'll dance in the moonlight,
I grow old, but why should I behave?

Oh show me a glade in the forest!
Where the fae and the sylphs still abide,
And in the grove dappled with sunlight,
I'll stroke the white hart's snowy hide.

Oh find me a desolate seashore!
Where I can commune with the sea,
And learn all the songs of the moon tides,
And finally learn to be me.

Oh give me the richness of cronehood!
For maiden and mother I've been,
I want to rewrite all my wrinkles
Before I sleep under the green.

The Demon List

I went to bed at half past one,
The list was almost halfway done
But then, it only lists by item...
Some jobs last *ad infinitum.*

Though that mid-point is false you see
But the illusion comforts me...
I can at least head off to bed
Without to-do lists in my head.

The list is long and just keeps growing
And there is no way of knowing
What will join the urgent pile
If I should let stuff wait awhile.

I have to be back up by six
To give the hound her morning fix
Of cool spring air and smells that lurk
Before I have to leave for work.

But could I sleep? No, could I hell,
My thoughts upon that list would dwell
No matter what I did or thought
My mind kept turning back to 'ought'.

So first, I tried to meditate,
And sent my conscious thoughts to wait
Where silent peace has made its vow
Within the chamber of 'not now'.

But did it work? For once, oh no,
My thoughts to silence would not go,

I shot the clock a narrowed look,
Then gave in and reached for a book.

But could I concentrate? Not yet.
I realised, with some regret
My thoughts, regardless of the time,
Just played around with silly rhyme.

And so, at half past two or three,
Just picture this... disgruntled me,
The bedside light switched on again
Armed with a notepad and a pen.

(And no, I know that doesn't rhyme,
But at this dark, unheard of time
An assonance will do just fine,
For just one small and measly line.)

I tried again, and then gave in,
Insomnia was going to win.
By four, I caved and just got up,
And headed for the coffee cup.

Downstairs the dog already waited,
Eagerness all unabated,
Ready for her morning run
And wanting me to share the fun.

There on the desk the demon lay,
The new to-do list for the day;
So please excuse me while I write...
I'd *really* like to sleep tonight!

The Archetypal Indie?

I don't have a feather to fly with...
Impecunious as a church mouse;
And to keep a roof over the keyboard,
I've sold half the stuff in the house.

The cupboards hold coffee and biscuits,
The fridge just an elderly egg,
But that's quite enough for survival,
I don't have to go out and beg.

See, I chose this career as a writer
And with painting a bit, as you do,
While still earning a crust at the day job,
I just about see the month through.

The house doesn't really need heating,
I really don't see it these days,
I just sit at the desk in the corner
While the words dance about in a haze.

On the other hand life's never boring!
As I roam through a new world each day,
When I wander through imagination
On a quest to find something to say.

And there's never the slightest dull moment,
No daydreaming, no time to yearn...
'Cause this Indie self-publishing model
Means always a new skill to learn.

I've learned how to edit and format,
I've gingerly learned how to prune,

And make cover pictures and promos
And dance to the Amazon tune...

As the night falls I'm burning the candles
When I should be tucked up in my bed,
I am still tapping words on the keyboard
And writing 'one more page' instead.

Is it worth it? You ask, so I'll tell you...
Over there on the shelf... take a look,
Sitting in pride of place in the corner
With my name on the spine of each book...

Fred

He strutted up and down the loft3
While puffing out his chest
Where iridescent feathers
Caught a rainbow on his breast.
The hens were all aflutter
'Cause they knew that Fred was King,
The undisputed champion
Who wore the racer's ring.
His picture hung upon the wall
His trophies on display,
And when the flock flew overseas
'Twas Fred would lead the way.
Blue-banded hunk, whose beady eye
Kept younger cocks in check,
Until the day he grew too old
And mother wrung his neck.
His coffin was a golden one,
A crispy pastry cave,
Bedecked with tender mushroom tops
More gravy, then, than grave.

Hair of the dog

I've washed the walls, and mopped
the soggy puddle off the floor
And cleaned the bathtub and the sink
and six foot up the door...
We had a bath, the dog and I,
before we went to sleep
Not both at once, that kind of lark
would make an angel weep!

Although I have to say
I might as well have just got in
I bathed her in my undies
and was soaked from neck to shin.
I've got to catch her first, you see,
she keeps me on my toes,
No matter what the stratagem,
the bugger always knows...

Another day she'll follow me
and wait beside the tub
And watch with curiosity
as I shampoo and scrub;
She knows my usual routine
and follows me inside...
Yet soon as she's the target
then she'll find somewhere to hide.

How does she know the water's running
nice and warm for her?
And that shampoo that's waiting
will be going in her fur?
It's not as if I bath her

very often if she's good...
But only when she's rolled about
in horrid, smelly mud.

I caught her... it was difficult,
'cause first I had to find her
Then carried her upstairs
and shut the bathroom door behind her.
She looked at me with deep reproach,
I knew she'd sulk and mope
Then wriggled like an octopus
and tried to eat the soap.

That awful moment's coming
when I have to let her go
And try to reach the towel,
but she doesn't want to know.
I try and dive and cover her
before she makes her break
But know full well regardless
that the small dog's going to shake.

By this time she is dripping,
and she's not the only one,
It's going to take hours
till the cleaning up is done.
For one small dog that shakes
can go an awfully long way...
I must be mad to bathe her
at this hour of the day.

When all is clean and tidy
then it's my turn for a treat,
And fragrant steam is rising
from the deep and scented heat
As I relax in luxury

the small dog wanders in
And watches my ablutions
with a really wicked grin.

I lie back for a soak and
then the rotten little mutt
Comes back and drops
a very muddy ball down by my foot.
The water's now disgusting,
she has won, the Ball of Power
Has made the bathtub filthy
and I have to have a shower.

I've had enough, and so I leave
my hair to dry alone,
The curly mop goes frizzy...
yes, I really should have known.
I'm way too old for ringlets..
and they stand out from my head...
I give up, turn the light off
and crawl wearily to bed.

I look a fright, I tell you,
but as if that weren't enough
The small dog's looking gorgeous
like a little ball of fluff.
The brown eyes still reproachful
as she settles for the night.
Her fur is feather soft,
a downy halo of delight.

Concede defeat, she's beaten me...
the small dog wins again.
I look like some mad harpy
with the curly, scarlet mane
A moral tail, you're asking?

Well, there is a point, at that...
If you're going to bathe a small dog
just be sure you have a hat.

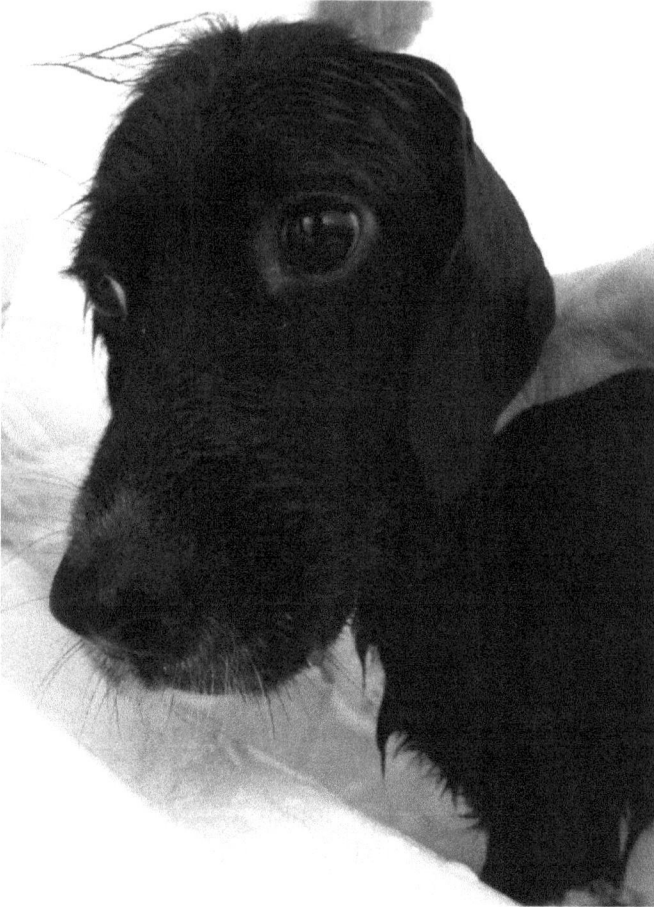

Mayhem and Black Coffee

It's just at the moment when everything's manic,
The clock's ticking fast and you're starting to panic,
Repeating your lines while the iron is steaming
And even for god's sake, when sleeping and dreaming...
That things unexpected will creep up and bite you
And minor disasters are starting to smite you.
Your email's gone down and you've run out of milk
And you're cursing the Microsoft men and their ilk,
The sewing machine has got all in a tangle
You fend off the dog and feel put through the mangle...
Both eyes swollen shut when you need to look decent
There's glue in your hair and it's probably recent.
The dog has acquisitive eyes on the cake
You've been trying all morning to get on and make;
The phone won't stop ringing, you're in a muck sweat
Your throat's closing up, but there's days to go yet...
Well, not many really for after tomorrow
What doesn't get done, you will beg, steal or borrow
The fumes from the glue make you feel a bit heady
But out in the kitchen the cake's nearly ready.
The wine glass looks tempting, but better not risk it,
Just stick to the coffee and maybe a biscuit....
Around you is mayhem, you're buzzing inside...
This weekend will be just one hell of a ride!
But you're going to make it... one more day ahead
So put down the cup and get working instead!

George and t' Dragon

"Nah, sithee," said Granny, "Just set thee dahn 'ere,
An' I'll tell the a tale old and true,
Of 'ow good Saint George slew a dragon one day
An' all dressed in a metal suit too.

It were like this..." she said as she warmed to her tale
With her listeners huddled around,
"The beast 'ad moved in and set up 'is abode
In a cave on the best 'unting ground.

The king weren't too pleased, it 'ad etten his 'oss
And the best of the royal deer too.
'To be fair,' said the mage, his opinion asked,
'What else would you expect it to do?'

'I've heard they like maidens,' his Majesty said,
'Give it one, then we'll be in the clear.'
'A maiden, my liege?' said the mage in surprise,
'Tha'll be lucky to find one round 'ere!'

The King scratched 'is head, there was something in that
'Cause for maidens... 'e'd known a fair few,
'We'll send out a search party over the land...
It'll give the lads something to do.'

The very next morning the lads all set off
All caparisoned, armoured and gay,
Trouble was, they were 'unting for pretty young maids
And wherever they found one, they'd stay.

Now the dragon had 'etten the rest of the deer
And had now set to work on the cows,

His Majesty went to his daughter and said,
'Hast thou kept all thy maidenly vows?'

'But of course, Dad!' she cried, 'I've had chance for nowt else
When I'm shut in this castle all day!'
'Just as well,' said the King, ' 'Cause we're in a reyt mess.
Get your coat and we'll be on our way.'

The princess was pretty with long golden hair,
The king thought he was onto a winner;
'Now just you 'ang on,' she said raising her chin,
'I can tell thee, I'm no dragon's dinner!'

Now t'lass were fed up being shut up inside
And was 'atching a plot of 'er own.
'I've got some conditions before we set off...
Get a pen, write it down... make it known'

Her Dad 'ad to do as his daughter prescribed
Though her orders were not what he'd like...
'Full half of my realm to your rescuer, lass?'
'Write it down, Dad, or just take a hike.'

He did as she said, then she patted his hand,
'Look, the rest of the plan's none so bad...
I'll marry him too, then you lose bugger all;
He can be the heir you never 'ad.'

She had a good point and the orders were read
Through the length and the breadth of the city.
But no-one stepped up, 'cause the dragon was big,
Even if the lass was rich and pretty.

There was only young George, at the tavern one night;
It were after bevy or seven,
His mates egged 'im on and he drunkenly said,

'Well, it sounds like a deal made in heaven.'

His pal were a blacksmith and all through the night
With the hammer and metal they clattered,
And made him a suit; though it rattled a bit,
That protected the assets that mattered.

He went to the king and his offer was met
With a fair bit of mocking and laughter;
'Is there anyone else 'ere who fancies the job?'
Asked the king... there was silence thereafter.

Now morning had come and poor George sobered up
And berated himself at 'is folly.
'Tha's no gumption, lad,' said his hungover head,
'And in fact, tha's an absolute wally.'

Too late to back out with the town at his feet
And the princess out there with the dragon,
'Now if tha survives,' the lad thought to himself,
'Georgie boy, tha must go on the wagon.'

The cave mouth looked dark as 'e rattled in close
And 'e knew that 'is chances were slim,
But with the town watching 'e had little choice
As 'e crept where the shadows were dim.

The suit was a pain and it chafed all the time
In some places 'e'd rather not mention,
George swore as he crept in the cavern's dark door
That from now on 'e'd stick to abstention.

The townsfolk looked on and the king wrung 'is hands
As the lad disappeared in the gloom.
They wondered how long they'd be waiting to see
If the lad really 'ad met his doom.

Strange noises were issuing out from the cave,
And the crowd winced and cringed as they listened,
Then out came the princess with George by her side
They were carrying something that glistened.

The folk never learned just what George found inside
And poor George was the only one knowing;
The princess was cooking a nice dragon stew
Over dragon-lit embers a-glowing.

'I skinned it,' she said, 'as the scales are quite tough,'
And George looked at the princess in horror.
'You might as well eat just to keep up your strength,'
She continued, 'You'll need it tomorrow.'

'Just do as I tell you and make no mistake
I will make sure they treat you right well,
But cross me just once,' she said waving her spear,
'Georgie boy, and I'll make your life hell.'

So they married next day amid feasting and joy
And the wine and the mead that flowed free,
But George just sat quiet and did as she bid,
Drinking naught but a nice cup of tea.

Not a drop touched his lips of the hard stuff that day,
And his manner seemed quiet and charming,
Yet under his breath he could be heard to pray
Which the courtiers found quite disarming.

'The man is reformed, hallelujah,' they said,
And they found his reserve to be quaint,
But the princess just smiled, knowing better than they
Just which dragon had made George a saint."

"Don't be daft, Granny, please," a dissenting voice said,
"That is not how they tell it at all."
"Oh no?" she replied, and they followed her gaze
To the dragonskin pinned on the wall.

The Mole

I'm pumped up on steroids and antibiotics,
At least, just for once they don't think I'm neurotic,
But do we have answers? Oh no, we do not,
They haven't the foggiest clue what I've got.

My blood pressure's fine, they are glad to report,
And all the mechanics seem just as they ought,
With doctorly skill and attentive detection,
They happily said they could find no infection.

Now, add in the headache, the aches and the pains,
And the bits that keep gurgling, rather like drains,
And the bits that won't move, and the bits that are stuck,
That when they get moving make me cry, 'Oh ****...'

Am I any wiser? Oh no, not a bit,
I'm not an antique yet, I'd rather be fit;
But this inflammation is taking its toll...
My eyes are so swollen I look like a mole.

No, not black and furry with velvety skin,
(Though that might be next, how does mole-dom begin?)
Now, this isn't funny, I hope you'll agree,
I'd even prefer looking something like me!

I've too much to do to be poorly, you know,
If it's going to do it, it might as well snow
Giving me a day off just to curl up in bed...
Though I'd probably just walk the small dog instead.

Wash 'n' go

I took a book into the bathtub today
It is something I used to like doing,
But over the past many years, I would say
I've grown expert at high speed shampooing.

'Me time' a concept that just passed me by
Or abandoned somewhere long ago...
What with fighting the sons for the bathroom each day
I just couldn't be bothered, you know.

But I had a day off so I dug out the treats
That were sent from way north of the border
I lined up the lotions and potions and stuff
For a beauty regime made to order.

The book waited patiently just within reach
While I turned from lobster to shrimp
And scrubbed and shampooed and perfumed and soaped...
Had a good girly preen and a primp.

I'd forgotten how long this lark takes, though you know
As I tended to each nook and cranny,
I began getting bored but my vanity said,
"That's no reason to look like your Granny!"

Now that was a good point, because Granny is dead
And although there are days when I feel it,
I'm still vain enough underneath this thick hide
To do anything to conceal it!

So I womanfully did my best for a while
Until I was bored with the bath,

Then I looked at the clock... twenty minutes had passed
And then really I just had to laugh.

So I rinsed the conditioner out of my hair
And noticed my fingers were crinkled...
And got out double quick when the thought crossed my
mind,
"Now I wonder what else will go wrinkled?"

And that, gentle reader, is why the book stayed
On the edge of the bathtub unread,
It's apparent my beauty regime's 'wash and go'
So I'll save all my reading for bed.

Doughnuts

I shall tell thee a tale o' when I were a lass
And came nobbut as 'igh as tha knee
When t'owd Yorkist Range were black-leaded and 'ot
And Great Granny was baking fer tea.

"Can I bake with you, Granny?" I asked smiling up,
"Nay lass, I'm in 'urry, tha' knaws...
'Cause when I'm done 'ere I mun polish yon floor,
Polish t'brasses and launder me drawers."

"What y' making?" I asked looking wistfully on
As the yeast started working in t'dough,
"Doughnuts," she said and I felt a bit peeved
'Cause I desp'rately wanted a go.

"Go see thee Grandad, he's out there in t'yard,
'Cause there's not enough space for thee 'ere."
So I went feeling glum to see what he were at
And if he'd 'ad a flea in 'is ear.

"What's mithering thee, little bairn," Grandad said
"'As ta bin chucked out 'ere just like me?
Come and lake out in t'garden , wi' me, lass, instead,
And we can mek doughnuts ... tha'll see!"

So he plonked dahn a shovel o' muck on the path,
And wi'water we mixed up the mud,
An' then we made doughnuts, all covered in worms
A bit messy, but by they looked good.

"And what 'as the pair of thee been lakin' at?"
Said Great Granny, with 'ands at her side,

"We've been makin' doughnuts," my Great Grandad said,
"Does t'a want one, lass?" "Nay, get inside!"

She muttered and mumbled while we washed our 'ands
And then we 'ad doughnuts and tea...
And from that day to this though it wasn't 'is name,
'Grandad Doughnuts' was 'is name to me.

Hearts and Flowers

I could send a Valentine greeting,
but you know, that is not on the cards,
I will just have to leave hearts and flowers
to all the romantics and bards.
There will not be a candlelit supper,
nor bottles of champagne on ice,
And it's too wet for moonlit romancing,
'cause in wellies you'd have to think twice!

There will not be a bouquet delivered,
no chocolates to go to my waist,
Nor a table for two in a corner
for dining with exquisite taste.
But don't think for a minute I'm lonesome,
I've got it all sussed, don't you see...
I'll just snuggle up by the fire
with a small dog asleep on my knee.

And her snores can replace gentle music,
then she'll look at me just in that way...
And I know that her mischief and laughter
will tell me I'm loved every day.
I don't need the cards and the flowers,
I don't need the satin and lace,
I only want eyes to laugh with me,
and a warm, open smile on a face.

It isn't about buying presents,
it isn't about what to do...
If just one day a year is for romance
then to me that is not loving true.
It's the ordinary moments that matter,

the sharing, the comfort, the love,
Not fluffy pink hearts on the one-day-a-year
all delivered by carrier-dove.

I remember the teenager watching
to see if the postman came through...
And the one dreadful year when he didn't...
and boy was that teenager blue!
For the day builds up this expectation,
and can leave us alone and forlorn
When you're waiting in vain for the postman,
who forgets you on Valentine's morn.

Just in case there is misunderstanding,
I'm a female as bad as the rest,
And a beautiful, romantic gesture,
will kindle the flame in my breast.
Yet a single red rose may be lovely,
but once cut it will never survive,
But a rose that is rooted securely in earth
will continue to flower and thrive.

But it needn't be champagne and roses,
it is easy to show that we care...
All it takes is a word or a touch or a smile
just to show that you want to be there.
For there is no *one* day when it matters
to show that the feeling is true...
It matters just knowing the one in your heart
holds a place in their heart just for you.

Ginger Nuts

I blame the hotel with its tea tray
So tempting just laid there, you know
While the shortbread could happily linger,
The ginger nuts just had to go.

I had made up a nice cup of coffee
To revivify me from the drive
For the road had been long since the morning
And I just couldn't wait to arrive.

Then all of a sudden I'd spied 'em,
All cellophane wrapped in their pack,
And once I had stretched out my fingers
I knew there'd be no turning back.

My Nemesis came back to haunt me
I never buy biscuits these days...
Not since the well dunked ginger biscuit
Became a gastronomic craze.

There's an art to this ginger nut dunking
Too little they're still hard to bite,
Too much and they splosh in the coffee
And drown like a ship in the night.

Then you have to look round rather quickly
To see if observers have seen,
Then fish with a half-eaten biscuit
To find where the fallen bit's been.

If you're skilful, or lucky, it's floating
And with a quite dexterous roll

Plunge the half eaten bit in to catch it
And swallow the soggy stuff whole.

But the slightest delay spells disaster
So you just have to give it your best...
You should have dived in their much faster,
As the half eaten bit joins the rest.

Now deep in the depths of your coffee
A ginger nut morass is lurking
And a last ditch attempt with the teaspoon
You can tell that it just isn't working.

Do you fish around coyly and chase it?
For if you do catch the absconder
You then need to think of disposal
And that is a fresh one to ponder...

Do you eat from the teaspoon naively?
And hope there is no-one to see?
Or clean off the spoon in a napkin,
Hidden furtively down by your knee?

Now this isn't so bad in your kitchen
Where no one can see what you've done...
But here in the posh hotel lobby
You just want to cut it and run.

But you can't, cause the ginger nut lurker
Is there in the depths of your cup,
Not so easy for you to dispose of
Even though you just drink it all up.

So you sit there and ponder the question
Do you drink and have dregs on display?
Or leave half the coffee still in there

And smile... walk politely away?

But if there is nobody watching
You could rinse the cup out with milk
All the while in the hope that observers
Will secretly be of your ilk.

You could of course be really sneaky
And wait for your friend to get up,
Then as they are leaving the table
Surreptitiously exchange the cup.

But not everyone gets so embarrassed
Though we British can be so uptight
That we happily dunk ginger biscuits
Then worry that it's impolite.

I can tell myself tales of all horrors,
And have nightmares of tea at the Ritz...
But that coffee and ginger confection
Will leave good intentions in bits.

And in spite of my stiff British manners
It is more than a question of taste...
When a whole pack of ginger nut biscuits
Takes up residence right on my waist.

See, for me the real problem is other
And although this 'ere text is predictive,
My problem with biscuits is simple..
Dunked ginger nuts are just addictive.

Brunch

Me and the dog had a sandwich for brunch
(Well, for me it was breakfast, for her it was lunch.)
She follows me into the kitchen like glue
Just in case I might rustle up something to chew.
You don't eat alone with a small dog in tow
And if you forget she will whine so you know
That she's starving to death, hasn't eaten in weeks...
Just so you'll believe her she'll suck in her cheeks
And manages somehow to look so pathetic,
With puppy-dog eyes that are purely cosmetic,
That there's no way you're eating that sandwich alone
Not unless in your breast beats a heart made of stone.
Now that's bad enough but there's worse on the menu
The kitchen, of course, is a wonderful venue
For practicing how to look thin and appealing
While keeping an eye out for something worth stealing.
She sits there observing me, testing my mettle
And licking her lips as I'm boiling the kettle
In dutiful mode I obey and I pour,
Put the small bowl of milk on her mat by the door,
She yawns and walks over and takes up position
And just to be cheeky looks up for permission
While keeping an eye out for possible plunder.
Just who is in charge here? I know you must wonder.
The answer is easy, when life seems a muddle
She's there with her head on your knee for a cuddle
And giving her love as the heart's true physician
While serving as some kind of weird dietician,
For when chips are down and you're feeling quite blue...
The small dog will happily eat the chips too.

An Author's Lament

I've decided on world domination,
It's a logical move, don't you think?
For it has to be better than housework
Or slaving away at the sink.

'Cause I've had it with laundry and cleaning,
After decades of doing the stuff,
And I've come to a point in the journey
Where I feel I should say, 'That's enough.'

I have much better use for my efforts,
I have daydreams I want to come true,
And there's no way that's going to happen
If I just sit and mope and feel blue.

So I sharpened my pen and my diction,
(And then chewed on its end for a while),
I should probably start writing fiction
Or perhaps ancient tales of the Nile?

Which is all very well but be honest,
There are thousands of stories out there...
So it's back to the drawing board thinking...
'Cause I must have a story to share.

So I stocked up on biscuits and coffee,
(In default of an IV infusion),
And debated the problem profoundly
In a dark state of bookish seclusion.

But meanwhile the dog joined the action
And she published a book of her own;

Now while she answers mail from her fan club
I go out for our walks all alone!

Perhaps I should publish the poems?
Though I wondered if they would be read...
But then Don and Wen were created...
So we wrote their adventures instead!

The story runs wild on the hilltops,
And mudslides in inclement weather,
And traces a mystical pathway
That laughingly leads through the heather.

We plunge deep into the Dark Ages,
And follow the hawks when they've flown,
We walk ancient tracks and chase symbols
That lead to the ley and the stone.

We're having such fun in the writing,
We travel the land far and wide,
(And diligently check the pubs out)
To find where the mysteries hide.

But to further the stated intention
And with world domination in view,
We need to be bestselling authors
To make all those daydreams come true.

But hang on, what's that in the email?
There's something I seem to have missed...
The first book I ever had published
Is up on a bestsellers list?

Now of course such success is illusion...
It was just a brief flash in the pan
But it just goes to show about daydreams...

If you dream you can do it... you can!

(*Author's note:* Just a small word of caution:
While such moments feel truly terrific...
When dreaming of world domination...
You really must be more specific!

The 'Bestselling Author' was lovely,
And 'Award Winning Poet' is too...
But your dreams must be really consistent
To make all your wishes come true!

So back to the keyboard, no shirking,
Or get down on your knees for reviews
And get that old grey matter working,
... And stay on good terms with your Muse!)

An earful of toothpaste.

I've stuffed my ear with toothpaste.
I gave up on other stuff,
But a mozzie in the earhole
Is the outside of enough.

I thought the things had finished,
Buggered off to hibernate,
But this voracious blighter
Seems as if it's running late.

I heard the whine... ignored it...
Because, if you remember
Summer's well and truly over
And we're almost in December.

I'd thought myself quite safe now...
Be a while before they're back...
But no, the damn thing got me
With an aerial attack.

My ear, of course, as happens,
When the mozzie comes to tea,
Immediately blossomed
Like a scarlet peony.

The antihistamines don't work...
Not pills, nor putting cream on,
It just swells up all virulent
And it itches like a demon.

The toothpaste is a last resort,
Not pretty, but effective,

Though as an ear adornment
Spearmint seems a tad defective.

Mosquito bites in winter
...Or at any time of year...
Are bad enough, but honestly
...Right in the bloody ear!

I had revenge, I have to say,
And no, I didn't swat it.
It flew across the small dog's view
So she just snapped and got it.

And so in spearmint misery
I'll just sit here and itch,
And write the mozzie's epitaph,
Put simply, "Death's a bitch."

Cold buttered toast

I had missed out on breakfast this morning,
And I'm not of the type to do brunch,
With my nose firmly glued to the keyboard
I completely forgot about lunch.

Now by mid-afternoon I was hungry
And so, with the small dog in tow,
I wandered off into the kitchen
To see where my fancy would go.

It's a bit of a bugger, I'm thinking,
As the cupboards all look a bit bare
And the fridge, though lit up and inviting,
Just looks back with its own vacant stare.

Never mind, there is cheese and the toaster
And that'll do nicely, says I,
But the cheese-hound has got there before me,
And stares back with an innocent eye...

There are eggs, and perhaps I could poach them?
That is, if they're fit for the toast;
They could have been lurking a while there
And be ready to give up the ghost.

I'm starving by this time, you'll gather,
The toast's going cold and won't wait;
So the microwave might be the answer
To get the damned things on the plate.

The moral to this little story,
And there has to be one, as you know,

Is to never put eggs in the zapper...
You'll be wearing your dinner 'to go'.

I'd remembered their dangerous habit
And pin-pricked them, thinking them fine,
But no... they exploded regardless
With the force of an organic mine.

Poor Ani dove under the cushions,
With her nose peeking out in dismay,
And the oven's been redecorated
With egg applied as a fine spray.

I'd forgotten, of course, till it happened
That the eggs would continue to cook,
They exploded again as I grabbed them,
And powdered egg's not a good look....

It sticks in your hair and your sweater,
And clings like the sea to the coast;
So I had a shower for dinner
And two bits of cold buttered toast.

Damned teenagers....

A range of smelly socks and pants
That decorate their room
An air of Gothic misery
Allied with doom and gloom...
The pre-dawn fumbling at the door
With keys that just won't go
Because (their tipsy minds assert)
The keyhole wobbles so...
Music (that defies the name)
Rebounding off the wall,
Yet they are quick to raise their voice
When Verdi's strains enthrall!
They are frustrating, noisy things
Of boundless appetite,
Who cannot put a loo seat down
Nor yet turn off a light!
And yet, when midnight catches me
For old loves lost with tears,
And memories return to haunt
The present with their fears,
When chips are down and bets are off
And life just seems a muddle
Its teenagers who give the love
And comfort of a cuddle.

Red Hair

I dyed my hair scarlet on Tuesday,
I admit that it doesn't look great...
But a glance in the mirror convinced me
That a girl really should celebrate!
No letters save bills on the doorstep,
No candlelit dinner awaited,
(And even a day or two later,
No envelopes postmarked 'belated'..)
A friend called to sing Happy Birthday!
(With words written 'specially for me!)
Then the phone went suspiciously silent
So I made chocolate gateau for tea.

I had thought of Great Granny that morning,
How she'd say as I braided her hair,
"I take twenty seven pills daily!'
Realising I'm half the way there!
I could dress in velvets and corsets,
Becoming an elderly Goth,
Or be a recycled teenager
In chintz with a vague hint of moth....
So, I dyed my hair scarlet on Tuesday,
Then regarded the scene of the crime,
As an aberrant act of rebellion
It had seemed the right thing at the time!

Sweet Briar

Now you've all heard the story about Briar Rose
Or you might know her best as Snow White;
The beautiful princess who wandered the woods
Who they say was all sweetness and light.

I have a complaint, she was not aptly named
If the girl was so shy and disarming;
I've wrestled with roses the whole afternoon
And believe me they're not ruddy charming.

A big briar rose had grown up through a bush
And like long ghostly fingers kept tapping,
Disturbing the dog with the intrusive sound
And awaking her when she was napping.

Now if she's asleep and awoken too quick
She will jump to her post to defend me,
That is all well and good when there's reason to bark
But a rose is supposed to be friendly.

So as all the blooms have now faded away
Out I went armed with bin bag and shears;
Within a few seconds I'm all tangled up
And it's got me from ankle to ears.

There is blood dripping down from a number of cuts
From the thorns that are savage and vicious,
The damn thing whips back and gets hold of my hair
With a grip that is downright malicious.

The dog who is watching all this through the pane
Then decides that her service is needed

And sets up a barking to waken the dead
While my shushing is going unheeded.

It's right at this moment the salesman arrives
And proceeds, with a smile, to deliver
His is well-practiced spiel with a confident air
Till he catches my eye with a shiver.

"I'll call back again," he says backing away
And I manage to answer politely,
That if he comes back he'll be well out of luck
And the dog can eat salesmen twice nightly.

It took me an hour to free myself then
From the briar's tenacious advances,
But blood-streaked and battered I cut the thing back
For the year... I was taking no chances.

So next time you read about sweet Briar Rose
Of her life and the way she preserved it,
Just ponder on this; if the girl's aptly named
There's a bloody good chance she deserved it!

Zombie Dawn

Why is it that on every day
when sleeping is a must
The Sandman overlooks
your daily dose of fairy dust?
Why does the night drag wakeful
when you need a decent slumber
And Insomniacs United
add your picture to their number?

You'd done the meditation
and the nice relaxing shower,
You'd had hot milk and read a bit
before the witching hour;
But still you lie there counting sheep,
the outcome undecided...
The day ahead is longer
than the sleep the night provided.

Alarm clocks are an insult
when they ring this time of morning,
Insanity to be up and going out
before the dawning!
You down another coffee
and the irony brings laughter,
You'd been so good but feel
like it's a lousy 'morning after'.

You'd fought for sleep and stayed awake
regardless all the night
And now you're drinking coffee
in the hope you'll be alright.

The moral of this story
told to your heart straight from mine?
Forget the malted bedtime milk,
and have a glass of wine.

Old Morpheus might then pop by
to join the celebration
And hold you in his sweet embrace
because of the libation.
You might as well... you feel as if
you're in the aftermath.
You've even shivered through
a rather bracing, chilly bath,
Had coffee on the doorstep
till the autumn turned you blue
... But the zombie in the mirror
looks an awful lot like you.

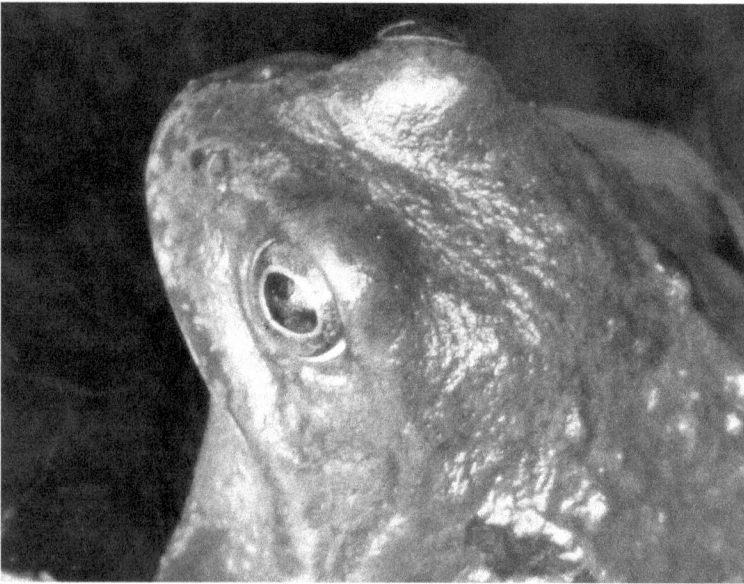

Homage

It was Albert that started the problem,
With his ill-fated 'osses 'ead stick
And Wallace, the somnolent lion,
Who swallowed the lad double quick.

I grew up on Marriott Edgar,
And the musket Sam wouldn't pick up,
And Lady Jane's ghost with the cold dripping toast
Not to mention the Chippendale Mupp.

Dr Seuss was a firm childhood favourite,
Spike Milligan took up the rear,
But I always returned to young Albert
And the stick stuck in Wallace's ear.

Yet it wasn't a frivolous pastime,
As history seeped in as well
And I learned about t' Battle of Hastings
In a way only Edgar could tell.

It isn't from school I remember
All the glorious tales of my land,
But from reading of Harold at Hastings
"On his 'oss with his 'awk in his 'and."

And then there was Magna Carta
The first ever human rights bill,
That was signed there on Runnymede Island
With King John who was looking quite ill.

"And it's through that there Magna Charter,
As were signed by the Barons of old,

That in England to-day we can do what we like,
So long as we do what we're told."*

So I learned all the words to recite them,
And for Granddad and Grandma I'd stand
And tell of old Sam and his musket,
Then they'd smile and say, "Eeh, that were grand."

'Cause poetry's rhyming and rhythm
Just takes up its home in your head,
And I'll probably still recite Albert
On the day I'm supposed to be dead.

I'll never be Wordsworth or Shakespeare,
But I notice a similar beat
In my verses to Marriott Edgar
And somehow that's really quite neat.

For the bards would have always shared laughter
As well as the history and stuff.
And if one of my ditties can stick in a brain
For the poet in me... that's enough.

*Verse quoted from Marriot Edgar's 'Magna Carta'

If you have enjoyed this book please consider leaving a review.
To contact the authors or to stay up to date with news of the books and
upcoming events, please request our newsletter by emailing:
suevincent@scvincent.com
You can also find us on Face book as Silent Eye Authors,
on Twitter @SCVincent
and on our website: www.franceandvincent.com

About the Authors

Sue Vincent is a Yorkshire born writer, esoteric teacher and Director of The Silent Eye. She has been immersed in the Mysteries all her life. Sue maintains a popular blog Daily Echo at www.scvincent.com and is the author of *The Osiriad* and *Sword of Destiny*, as well as a number of books with Stuart France.

Sue lives in Buckinghamshire, having been stranded there some years ago due to an accident with a blindfold, a pin and a map. She has a lasting love-affair with the landscape of Albion, the hidden country of the heart. She is currently owned by a small dog who also blogs.

The friendship of Vincent and France has a peculiar alchemy of humour, scholarship and vision that has given birth to several books, including *The Initiate, Heart of Albion* and *Giants Dance*.

The Silent Eye is a modern Mystery School that seeks to allow its students to find the inherent magic in living and being. With students around the world the School offers a fully supervised and practical correspondence course that explores the self through guided inner journeys and daily exercises. It also offers workshops that combine sacred drama, lectures and informal gatherings to bring the teachings to life in a vivid and exciting format. Full details of the School may be found on the official website: www.thesilenteye.co.uk

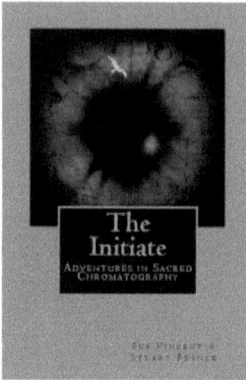

THE INITIATE:

Adventures in Sacred Chromatography

Sue Vincent & Stuart France

Foreword by Steve Tanham

Book One of the Triad of Albion

Imagine wandering through an ancient landscape wrought in earth and stone, exploring the sacred sites of peoples long ago and far away in time and history. The mounds and barrows whisper legends of heroes and magic, painted walls sing of saints and miracles and vision seeps through the cracks of consciousness.

Now imagine that the lens of the camera captures a magical light in soft blues and misty greens and gold. A light that seems to have no cause in physical reality. What would you do?

If you were open to the possibility of deeper realities, perhaps you would wish to explore this strange phenomenon...something two people came to know as sacred chromatography.

The Initiate is the story of just such a journey beyond the realms of our accustomed normality. It is a factual tale told in a fictional manner. In this way did the Bards of old hide in the legends and deeds of heroes those deeper truths for those who had eyes to see and ears to hear.

As the veils thin and waver, time shifts and the present is peopled with the shadowy figures of the past, weaving their tales through a quest for understanding and opening wide the doors of perception for those who seek to see beyond the surface of reality.

Over 60 Full Colour Illustrations

THE HEART OF ALBION:

Tales from the Wondrous Head

Stuart France & Sue Vincent

Book Two of the Triad of Albion

"If I am consciously following a woman who is about to engage a Llama in conversation, which I certainly appear to be, it does not impinge too negatively upon my thought processes."

What do Jack and the Beanstalk have to do with a spiritual quest? What, for that matter, is the nature of the relationship between Salome and the Jester? Why is Wen conversing with a llama in the Yorkshire Dales? And what links the beautiful and sacred landscape that is the Heart of Albion with Breakfast in Slug Town? These, and many other questions, must be considered as Don and Wen continue the journey begun in The Initiate exploring the shadowy roots of the ancient myths and legends of these Blessed Isles, steering a perilous path through the murky waters of religious symbolism and iconography.

"Breakfast in Slug Town?"

Join them on their continuing quest for knowledge and understanding as they explore the landscape of England and people it with strange creatures and even stranger theories, using sacred intent and guided imagination to penetrate into the mysteries unfolding before them.

Illustrated in full colour throughout

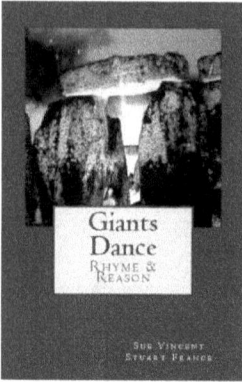

GIANTS DANCE:

Rhyme and Reason

Stuart France and Sue Vincent

Book Three of the Triad of Albion

It began with a walk over the bracken covered hillsides of Derbyshire to a lonely stone circle, almost forgotten. It was just a walk...until the hawk flew from the tree and once again the visions began.

Plunged into a realm beyond reality, further than history, deeper than time, Don and Wen begin to unravel the hidden messages hidden in plain sight, concealed by habit and acceptance, and extraordinary magic framed within the small things of ordinary life.

Follow a journey across the Heart of Albion and become an Initiate of the mysterious verity of verse.

"Interesting that they should seek to make the seven four like that."

"Three harmonic pairs and a jubilant head?"

"It reminds me of something biblical."

"It wouldn't be Jubilees would it? The Hebrews, you know, took an awful lot with them when they fled from Egypt."

"I know, but it's not Jubilees, although that does bear some consideration. It's the three-score years and ten! It's precisely the same dynamic. In fact, we even raised the question of whether there was anything in the tradition appertaining to it."

"And now we have our answer!"

"The Hebrew's Divinely sanctioned earthly span of life is determined by the Seven Hathors."

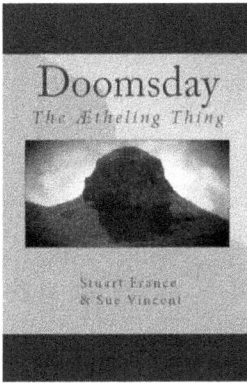

Book One of the Doomsday Triad

Doomsday: The Ætheling Thing

Stuart France & Sue Vincent

"Who was this Arviragus bloke anyway?"

Don studies the light as it plays through his beer, casting prisms on the table. How is it possible to hide such a story… the hidden history of Christianity in Britain? Oh, there are legends of course… old tales… Yet what if there was truth in them? What was it that gave these blessed isles such a special place in the minds of our forefathers? There are some things you are not taught in Sunday School.

***

"Get this… 'ætheling from O.E. Æpling, 'son of a king, man of royal blood, nobleman, chief, prince, king, Christ, God-Man, Hero, Saint…"
"Wait a minute… wait a minute… give me that last bit again."
"…Christ, God-Man, Hero, Saint…"
"Didn't we call our Arthur, Aeth in, 'The Heart of Albion'?"
"We did."
"And didn't we set his story in Mercia?"
"We did."
"Well that's it then…The Anglo Saxon kings were claiming divine descent."
"That's true, but the Anglo-Saxon kings' descent wasn't from God it was from Christ."
"And how did they get there?"
"They got there from their very own High One who also hung from a tree with a spear in his side… screaming."
"Odin!"
"They evidently regarded Christ as an avatar of Odin."
"Blimey, you'll not read that in any history book!"
"Just as well we're not writing a history then isn't it?"

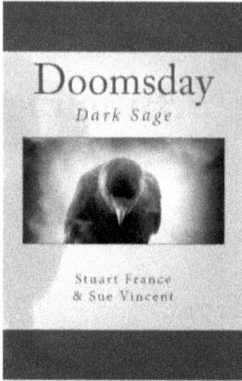

Doomsday: Dark Sage

Stuart France & Sue Vincent

.... something was spawned up on the moor... something black that flew on dark wings...It heeds not time or place...It seem to have developed a penchant for the travels of Don and Wen....

"Are those two still at it?"
"Apparently...."

The Dark Ages appear in the copybook pages of our historical records like an ink spot. An insidious black mark; a veritable blot on the landscape of time. There are some who claim they never actually existed and that the two hundred odd years represented by their darkness are a fabrication designed to fit the grandiose plotting of an ego-driven king. There are probably only two people mad enough to take such a notion seriously.

Across the Derbyshire landscape, scattered with sites of ancient sanctity and strange, otherworldly places, our two unlikely companions begin another chapter of their quest to understand the roots of human consciousness and the source of inner light that draws the eyes and heart towards to sun.

SWORD OF DESTINY

Sue Vincent

"...and the swords must be found and held by their bearers lest the darkness find a way into the heart of man. Ask the waters to grant guidance and tell the ancient Keeper of Light that it is time to join battle for the next age."

Rhea Marchant heads north to the wild and beautiful landscapes of the Yorkshire Dales where she is plunged into an adventure that will span the worlds. The earth beneath her feet reveals its hidden life as she and her companions are guided by the ancient Keeper of Light in search of artefacts of arcane power. With the aid of the Old Ones and the merry immortal Heilyn, the company seek the elemental weapons that will help restore hope to an unbalanced world at the dawn of a new era.

" Sue writes with a real grasp of the human side of people which is expressed in the personalities of her heroes and the recognizable characters that they interact with. The power and essence of her story is found in the admixture of her undoubted love of Yorkshire, her ability to see the warm and the good in all people, and her knowledge of the magical forces one can find at work in such places and between such folk. An inspired piece of writing that keeps your attention until the very last page."

Dr G.M.Vasey, author of "The Last Observer" and "Inner Journeys: Explorations of the Soul ", co-author of "The Mystical Hexagram: The Seven Inner Stars of Power".

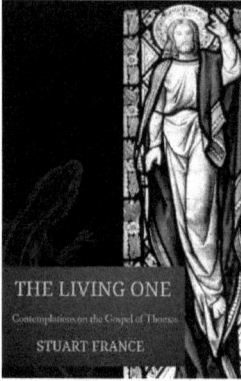

THE LIVING ONE:

Contemplations on the Gospel of Thomas

Stuart France

"...It is like the smallest of seeds and if it falls on prepared soil, it produces the largest of plants and shelters the birds of heaven..."

Many scholars believe that the Gospel According to Thomas preserves a glimpse into the oral traditions of the Gospels. The book is a collection of sayings, parables and dialogues attributed to Jesus and forms part of the Nag Hammadi Library, a collection of ancient papyri found near the Dead Sea in 1945.

In this unique interpretation Stuart France brings the oral tradition to life, retelling the Gospel in his own words, in the way it may have been shared around the hearth fires of our forefathers. Deeply entwined with the story is the personal journey to understanding, following it down some rather unusual pathways. It begins with a road trip in an arid landscape far from home; a journey that led through a country that captured imagination and set it to music. It ends with an ancient story, told as you have never read it before.

"Look, it's obvious, mozzies are God's Angels in disguise."

Accompanied by a commentary which draws upon the esoteric traditions of the Mystery Schools, The Living One provides a new window on an age old story, being a transmutation of the spirit of the words, born of the personal realisations of a seeker after Truth.

> **"Salome said to Joshua, "Who are you mister, you have eaten from my table and climbed on to my couch as if you are a stranger ?"**

Photography by Sue Vincent

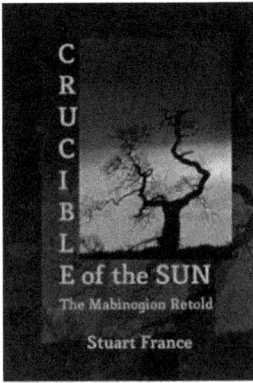

CRUCIBLE OF THE SUN:

The Mabinogion Retold

By Stuart France

"I will dazzle like fire, hard and high, will flame the breaths of my desire; chief revealer of that which is uttered and that which is asked, tonight I make naked the word."

Once upon a time we gathered around the flames of the hearth and listened to tales of long ago and far away. The stories grew in the telling, weaving ancient lore whose origins lie somewhere in a misty past with tales of high adventure, battles, magic and love. In Crucible of the Sun this oral tradition is echoed in a unique and lyrical interpretation of tales from the Mabinogion, a collection of stories whose roots reach back into the depths of time, spanning the world and reflecting universal themes of myth and legend.

These tales capture a narrative deeply entwined through the history of the Celtic peoples of the British Isles, drawing on roots that are embedded in the heart of the land. In Crucible of the Sun the author retells these timeless stories in his own inimitable and eminently readable style. The author's deep exploration of the human condition and the transitions between the inner worlds illuminate this retelling, casting a unique light on the symbolism hidden beyond the words, unravelling the complex skein of imagery and weaving a rich tapestry of magic.

Photography by Sue Vincent

'The author's creative and scholarly engagement with the material and enthusiasm for the original tales is evident throughout.' The Welsh Books Council

'I found it very inspiring!' Philip Carr-Gomm, Chosen Chief, Order of Bards, Ovates and Druids (O.B.O.D.)

THE OSIRIAD
Isis & Osiris, the Divine Lovers

Sue Vincent

"There was a time we did not walk the earth. A time when our nascent essence flowed, undifferentiated, in the Source of Being."

In forgotten ages, the stories tell, the gods lived and ruled amongst men. Many tales were told, across many times and cultures, following the themes common to all mankind. Stories were woven of love and loss, magic and mystery, life and death. One such story has survived from the most distant times. In the Two Lands of Ancient Egypt a mythical history has been preserved across millennia. It begins with the dawn of Creation itself and spans one of the greatest stories ever to capture the heart and imagination. Myths are, by their very nature, organic. They grow from a seed sown around a hearth fire, perhaps, and the stories travelled the ancient highways, embellished and adapted with each retelling. Who knows what the first story told?

In this retelling of the ancient story it is the Mistress of all Magic herself who tells the tale of the sacred family of Egypt.

"We have borne many names and many faces, my family and I. All races have called us after their own fashion and we live their stories for them, bringing to life the Universal Laws and Man's own innermost heart. We have laughed and loved, taught and suffered, sharing the emotions that give richness to life. But for now, I will share a chapter of my family's story. One that has survived intact through the millennia, known and remembered still, across your world. Carved in stone, written on papyrus, I will tell you of a time when my name was Isis."

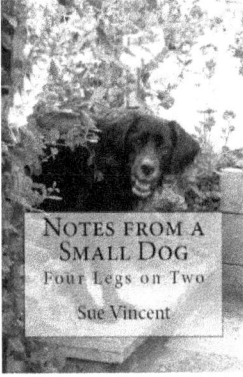

NOTES FROM A SMALL DOG

Four Legs on Two

Sue Vincent

"He asked me what it is with balls…why I love them so much. I had a think about that. It is 'cause they fly. Like birds. I'm supposed to chase birds. I'm a bird-dog. 'Course, she won't really let me. It doesn't stop me barking at 'em and seeing 'em off from my garden. But it isn't the same. Somewhere, deep inside, I know what I am supposed to do, what I am supposed to be. But I can't be that for some reason… things aren't quite set up right for me to chase birds all day and bring them back to her. On the other hand, that's who I am…and you can't be anything else than that… so the balls let me be myself in a world where I can't catch birds all day.

She says that's not unusual… She seems to think that we all know who we really are, deep down, and that we spend all our time trying to find a way to be that in a world that doesn't quite seem to fit. We either find other stuff to express it…like balls…. Or we try and be what others think we should be… But you can't be a terrier if you are a retriever, can you? A bit like asking a fish to climb trees. It can be done, but it isn't easy!"

Ani, a very familiar spirit, was named for one of the ancient gods. It should, I suppose, have been no surprise when she took over the keyboard and began to write. A year later she had me collect her writings into a single volume at the insistence of her fans… who have been taken by her playful love of life and her odd wisdom…largely because she is saving for an automatic tennis ball launcher. The book is a collection of Ani's periodic posts. She even lets me write occasionally… By this time you may, of course, think I am barking mad myself… you may have a point… but I stand with Orhan Pamuk, "Dogs do speak, but only to those who know how to listen."

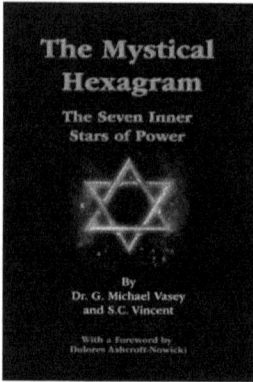

THE MYSTICAL HEXAGRAM:

The Seven Inner Stars of Power

Dr G. Michael Vasey & S.C.Vincent

Foreword by Dolores Ashcroft-Nowicki

The Mystical Hexagram is a new book by Dr G. Michael Vasey and S.C.Vincent. The book explores a symbol. Not from some scholarly or deeply complex perspective, but seeing it as a representation relating to life and living. The forces and pressures that are associated with the hexagram are, after all the forces of life at both practical and Universal levels. By exploring and beginning to understand the symbol, we are able to learn and discover more about ourselves.

The meditations throughout the book take you on an inner journey of exploration, discovering the parallels between the self and the greater reality within which we live our lives. They illustrate the connection between the inner and outer world of the self and the cosmic forces of Creation. Having traced that connecting path, the meditations offer a practical way of applying that understanding.

In addition to the exercises the book includes two very special meditations, The Garden of Remembrance and the Circle of Healing. These two you will want to revisit many times, taking away from the experience a sense of peace and beauty.

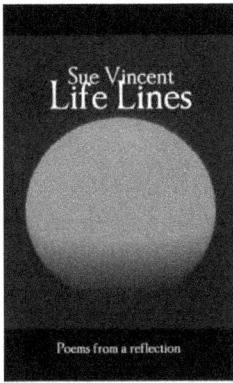

LIFE LINES:

Poems from a Reflection

Sue Vincent

A collection of fifty-two poems of life, love and inspiration.

There are joys for which we cannot find expression, moments that have a depth of emotion that can only be shared in images. It is here that poetry comes into its own, for the pictures we paint with words can conjure all the emotions of the human heart. From solitude to passion, from aspiration to the quest for the soul's inner light, we seek to find ways to share our journey through life, to witness our footsteps as we pass through its shifting sands and cast a reflection on time itself. The poet is both mirror and reflection, framing the images of a human life and giving them a beating heart.

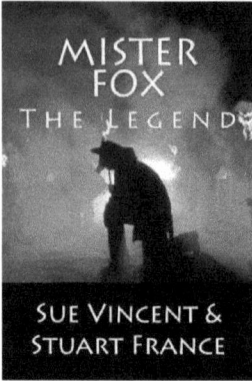

MISTER FOX: THE LEGEND

Sue Vincent & Stuart France

A Graphic Novel

Where do they come from?
They come out of the night…
Where do they go to?
Back to the night they return…
They dance in the dark to pipe and drum and fiddle
They dance in the dark with fire and brandished flame…

No-one knows who they are…

But why do they dance?
What is the story behind this magical spectacle?
There are rumours, legends…
Don and Wen set out to investigate.
In a darkened corner of the Waggon and Horses, Langsett, a hooded and enigmatic figure whispers secrets…

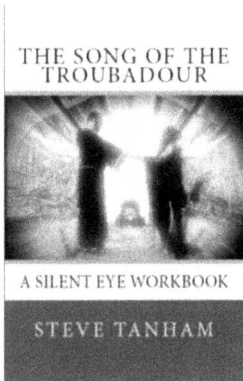

THE SONG OF THE TROUBADOUR:

A Silent Eye Workbook

by Steve Tanham

Foreword by Sue Vincent

With contributions from Stuart France and those who were there to share this very special journey.

"Being is without beginning and end. This flowing, loving, intelligence is the basis of everything we know. Whatever level of consciousness we attain, it will only reveal the greater and greater depth of Being that has always been there within us and before us.

Being also forms the objects that we believe are separated from us. But the Reality and the Truth are that we live and have our own being in a sea of endless loving energy that is our true home. There is no separation, there is in the end, no journey; there is only realisation, and seeing. What unveils itself before us was always there."

A group of pilgrims have been brought together in the ancient monastery of the Keepers of the First Flame. Unexpectedly, the door opens and into their midst stride the Troubadours, holding a Child by the hand…. a very special Child in whom the Light of Being shines clear… and who can see the world as it really is…

Thus began the inaugural weekend that saw the Birthing of the Silent Eye, a modern Mystery School. This workbook is both a practical transcript of the dramatic rituals of that weekend and the story of that Birth. The book opens a window onto the workings of a modern Mystery school, sharing the accounts of some of those who attended the weekend as well as the detailed script of the powerful ritual drama. If you have ever wondered what really goes on… this book is for you.

Land of the Exiles

A Silent Eye Workbook

With Practical Notes

By Steve Tanham

With Contributions from Sue Vincent and Stuart France

and the Companions of the Hawk.

In April 2014 the Silent Eye, a modern Mystery School, hosted the Land of the Exiles as a weekend workshop. These annual gatherings attract people from across the world to share a unique approach to the spiritual journey that is taken by all. Over the course of the workshop a story unfolds, dramatic and emotive, engaging the hearts and minds of the participants, shadowing forth the challenges of the inner journey to awakening. This workbook includes the script from that journey, along with practical and explanatory notes, as well as the personal accounts of some of the Companions who shared an epic journey of the imagination as a spaceship crash-lands on a far-flung planet, and a cyborg forces them to play out the story of the ancient gods of Egypt, intent of calculating just what it means to be human…

The Hawk has crash-landed on the planet Idos, the crew awake from cryogenic sleep to find that their captain is missing and the ship has been taken over by a cyborg who bends them to his will, making them play out the stories of the ancient gods of Egypt as it seeks to understand what it is to be human. Their only hope of survival lies in the strange touch of the Midstream, and their own inner hearts.

A practical guide to a fully scripted ritual workshop from the Silent Eye, a modern Mystery School.

www.ingramcontent.com/pod-product-compliance
Lightning Source LLC
Chambersburg PA
CBHW060530030426
42337CB00021B/4201